Explore Music through Movement

David Wheway and Shelagh Thomson

17 varied national curriculum Music activities linked to the P.E. attainment targets

Music Department
OXFORD UNIVERSITY PRESS
Oxford and New York

Oxford University Press, Walton Street, Oxford OX2 6DP, England

Oxford is a trade mark of Oxford University Press

First published 1993

ISBN 0 19 321874 7

Design and illustration by Creative Intelligence, Bristol

Printed in Great Britain by Caligraving Ltd., Thetford, Norfolk

Contents

4 **Introduction**

List of Activities

8 Stop/Go
9 Elephants and Mice
10 Reflections
11 The Locomotion
12 Charley Marley
13 Catching/Rolling
14 'Dumm-Clop'
15 Rollerball
16 Scramble
17 Make a Folk Dance
18 Warm Up
19 Mirror Mirror
20 The Hidden Doorway
21 Twister
22 Get Together
23 Choreography
24 Sound Moves

Appendix

25 Glossary
26 Pentatonic Scales

There are nine books in this series;

Explore Music through

Art, Geography, History, Maths, Movement, Poetry and Rhyme, Science, Stories, Word Games.

Introduction

These booklets are designed for primary teachers who value the role of music in an integrated approach to the curriculum. They are of equal value to those who have little or no experience of teaching music, or those who have responsibility as a music co-ordinator.

By closely relating musical activities to other areas of the curriculum, it is hoped that primary teachers will feel more confident when engaging in musical activities with children.

Within each of the nine booklets in the series, activities are ordered progressively from 'early years' through to upper Key Stage 2.

The appropriateness of any activity will depend on the previous experience of the child or group. For this reason we have not recommended any activity for a specific age group, but have indicated a target Key Stage.

Many activities, especially those primarily concerned with composition, are often best delivered over a number of sessions. This allows time for exploratory work, and also for evaluation, discussion, and development.

Building a Repertoire of Sounds

Children need an ever-increasing knowledge of sounds, and teachers need to be aware of the importance of sound exploration for future musical activities. This repertoire of sounds is especially important when children wish to represent feelings, objects, and other sounds in their compositions.

Body and Vocal Sounds

Children should explore the possibility for sounds made both vocally and with the body. For instance, how many sounds can be made with the throat? ('Ooooh', 'Ahhhh', a hiccup, a cough, a gargle, humming, sighing, panting, etc.) What different sounds can be made by patting different parts of the body? (Cheeks, chest, stomach, thighs, knees, etc.)

Classroom Percussion

Children should be encouraged to find as many different ways as possible to play percussion. Can it be scraped, tapped, shaken, scratched, blown, etc.? When a new sound is found, think about what moods or images it conjures up. Such exploration works well in small groups, using a limited number of instruments. Allow the children time to play new sounds to the rest of the class.

Percussion Resources

Some considerations when building resources:

Do your percussion resources offer a wide choice for creating a variety of sounds?

Are the instruments made from a variety of materials (e.g. wood, metal, plastic, etc.)?

Does the collection contain instruments from different ethnic origins?

Are the instruments of good quality? Remember, as in other areas of the curriculum, poor quality materials (e.g. worn or broken) may lead to poor or disappointing results.

Other Sound Makers

A wide variety of sounds can be made with everyday objects such as paper, kitchen utensils, beads and pulses (e.g. paper tearing, scrunching, flapping; pulses poured into a bucket, swirled around, shaken; pots and pans drum-kit).

When performing any activity, try different combinations of sound, as this adds to the children's exploratory work, and their understanding of timbre and texture.

Recording

It is very important that children develop ways of recording their compositions. A variety of ways are suggested throughout the booklets, for example, pictures, symbols, words, letters, and so on. Ensure paper and appropriate recording materials are always available.

Audio as well as video recorders are also valuable resources for recording children's work and development.

The Activities

Suggested Materials

These materials should be useful as a guide for preparing the lessons. They are only suggestions and teachers may wish to select their own materials.

Suggested Listening

Generally, it is a good idea to keep extracts short, e.g. 30–60 seconds in duration. If possible, tape-record extracts beforehand to avoid searching in the lesson.

Most of the suggestions given are easily available in record libraries or through record shops. Many can be found on compilations. Where this is not the case, a reference is given.

The recordings we have recommended should not be considered either obligatory or comprehensive.

Personal collections of recorded music are a valuable resource. However, do avoid limiting the children's listening opportunities to any one type of music.

Attainment Target Boxes

The left-hand box gives an indication of the main focus of each activity, relating to the national curriculum for Music. However it should be noted that the activities will also offer a variety of other musical experiences.

The right-hand box indicates how the activity may complement work undertaken in another area of the curriculum.

Classroom Organization

For many whole-class activities, a circle of children on a carpet or chairs is ideal. This helps concentration and promotes a feeling of involvement, as well as being practical when it comes to observing other children, whole-group involvement, and passing games. It might be advisable at times to split the class or set into groups.

There are some activities that require little or no percussion, and if you are just starting out you may feel more confident attempting these activities initially.

Handing Out Instruments

Avoid the children making a headlong rush to the music trolley at all costs! Allow the children to collect, or hand out, a few instruments at a time.

- Have the required instruments placed out ready beforehand.
- While listening to instructions, children should place their instruments on the floor in front of them.
- Give out beaters for instruments last.

- Before commencing agree on clear signals for stopping and putting instruments down (e.g. a hand in the air, a finger to the lips, a wink of the eye, etc.).
- Demand an immediate response to these signals.
- Encourage children to treat instruments with respect at all times. (This is not easy if instruments are worn or broken.)

Evaluation and Appraisal

When children are working on a composition, there should be regular evaluation by the teacher, and/or by the children, of how the work is progressing. This will include a great deal of purposeful listening and appraising. The process will in turn help the children in appraising the music of others.

Key Questions for Performers and Audience

Can you tell us about your music?

How did the piece start/finish?

What did you like about it?

What contrasts/changes did the piece contain?

Does the piece fulfil the task set?

Was it performed fluently and appropriately?

Could it have been improved, and if so, how?

Could the piece be extended, and if so, how? (e.g. repetition, contrasts, new material, different instruments, etc.)

Did the audience listen well?

Stop/Go

Suggested Materials

A selection of percussion instruments.

This is a very simple listening activity which can be incorporated into a movement session with young children.

1. Choose an instrument to play, and discuss with the children what kind of movement would match the sound, e.g.

   tambourine shaken – whirling and twirling
   slow, low drumbeat – low, wide, slow, stretching movements.

2. Decide on two sounds and the movements to go with them. Ensure the children cannot see what you play. They should listen carefully and respond with the appropriate movement when an instrument is being played, but freeze when it stops.
3. Gradually build up the number of sounds (and therefore movements) that you use in the activity. Try to encourage careful listening and an immediate response.
4. Hand out percussion instruments to some of the children. These instruments should be the same as in 1 – 3. The children with instruments take it in turns to play, while the other children take turns to demonstrate the appropriate movement.

   Alternatively, a child without an instrument demonstrates a movement, and the child with the appropriate instrument plays.

Music Attainment Target: 2 Main Focus: Listening Key Stage: 1	P.E. Attainment Target: 1 Main Focus: Movement

Elephants and Mice

Suggested Materials

Drum

1. Ask the children to think about the largest animal they know. Usually an elephant will be mentioned. Talk about the way an elephant walks – slowly, heavily, etc.
2. Play slow, loud footsteps on a drum, and ask the children to move like elephants to the drumbeat – starting when it starts, stopping when it stops.
3. What small animals do they know of? Talk about mice. How do they move? – quickly, lightly, etc.
4. On the drum play light, fast beats and repeat the activity with the children moving this time like mice.
5. Now vary what you play, sometimes the elephant beats, sometimes the mice. Encourage the children to listen carefully and respond with the appropriate movement.
6. Discuss other animals with the children. Can they think of one that walks faster than an elephant but slower than a mouse (e.g. a donkey)?

   Incorporate this animal into the activity so that there are three speeds for the children to identify and respond to.

Extension Activities

Ask the children to sit in a circle. One by one the children go into the middle and choose one of the animals' movements to perform. The other children, using their knees as drums, accompany the movement.

(Some of the children might like to find sounds on other percussion instruments that remind them of particular animals.)

Music Attainment Target: 2
Main Focus: Listening and Pace
Key Stage: 1

P.E. Attainment Target: 1
Main Focus: Movement

Reflections

Suggested Listening

Recordings of music with a clear pulse, for example pop music.
(BBC tapes for movement programmes can be useful.)

1. The children sit in a circle, or in a position where they can all see the leader.
2. The leader responds to the pulse of the music with a repeated action, e.g.

    tapping on head
    patting knees
    moving thumbs up and down, etc.

3. The children copy the leader, who changes the action regularly once the majority of children are responding accurately.
4. When the activity is well established the children might like to take it in turns to be the leader.

It is useful to do this activity to extracts of music with a variety of tempos. Discuss the change in pace with the children.

(Responding to a slow pulse is very hard for young children, but a very useful activity as it demands a lot of control and concentration.)

Songs the children know well can also be used.

This activity is a good warm up for music sessions.

Music Attainment Target: 1
Main Focus: Pulse
Key Stage: 1

P.E. Attainment Target: 1
Main Focus: Movement

The Locomotion

Suggested Materials

Tambour or drum. Vocal/body sounds.

Suggested Listening

After completion of the activity the children could listen to *Pacific 231* by Honegger.

1. Ask the children to listen while you tap a drum or a tambour very slowly. Gradually speed your beats up, then slow them down again.

2. Can the children describe what has happened to the beats?

3. Children find a space and then respond to your playing by walking faster/slower. This will need careful listening and practice.

4. When this activity has been established, have children lead by playing the drum.

5. Spend some time with the children exploring ways in which they could move like trains.

6. The children now move around the hall, to a short movement story, e.g.

a) The train is still.
b) The train pulls slowly out of the station.
c) The train picks up speed, then maintains it for a while.
d) The train slows going up a steep hill.
e) The train speeds up again.
f) The train slows down, and pulls into a station.
g) The train is still.

7. Some children might like to provide vocal/body sound accompaniment, e.g. rubbing hands, puffing.

8. Can the children find other interesting sounds that could be incorporated, maybe on percussion instruments?

Music Attainment Target: 2
Main Focus: Appraising and Pace
Key Stage: 1

P.E. Attainment Target: 1
Main Focus: Movement

Charley Marley

Suggested Materials

Rhyme, as below.

1. In the playground the children often chant rhymes to which they put a 'pat-a-cake' accompaniment. The children face each other in pairs and build up a sequence of clapping using their own and their partners' hands to clap against. Other movements such as slapping thighs can also be included.
2. This type of activity can be added to any rhyme with a strong rhythmic 'feel', such as 'Charley Marley':

   Charley Marley
   Stole some barley
   Out of a baker's shop.
   The baker came out
   And gave him a clout
   Which made poor Charley hop!

3. Encourage the children to work on the movements until they can produce a clear, rhythmic, and fluent performance of the rhyme. Children might find their own rhyme and devise their own accompaniment for it.
4. Do the children know any other action rhymes that they could share with the class?

Music Attainment Target: 1
Main Focus: Rhythm
Key Stage: 1/2

P.E. Attainment Target: 1
Main Focus: Co-ordination

Catching/Rolling

Suggested Materials

A selection of balls. Pitched percussion instruments.

This is a very simple listening game to encourage pitch discrimination which could be incorporated into P.E. sessions on ball skills.

1. Children face each other in pairs, with one ball between each pair.
2. If the teacher, using pitched percussion or piano, plays a high note, the children must **throw** the ball to their partner. If, however, the teacher plays a low note, the children must **roll** the ball to their partner.
3. The difficulty of this activity can be controlled:
   - physically – altering the size of the balls and the space between the children
   - musically – altering the distance between the two notes you choose to represent high and low. (The hardest would be notes next door to each other.)

Extension Activities

Extend this activity for older children by asking the children to listen to a sequence of notes carefully, and then do the appropriate actions afterwards, e.g.

Teacher plays: high, high, high, low

Children then: throw, throw, throw, roll

You may like to add a middle note which the children could then represent by throwing while kneeling.

Music Attainment Target: 2 Main Focus: Pitch Key Stage: 1/2	P.E. Attainment Target: 1 Main Focus: Ball Skills

'Dumm-Clop'

Suggested Materials

One ball per child.

Suggested Listening

Music with a fairly slow, clear, steady pulse. Some recordings of pop music, or 'swing' might be appropriate. Ravel's *Boléro* is also good for this activity.

This activity only takes a short time, and is useful to include in a lesson on ball skills.

1. Play the music to the children and ask them to clap along to the pulse.
2. Each child now has a ball, and tries to bounce and catch their ball in time to the music. (This is not as easy as it sounds and will require practice.)
3. If a child does not catch their ball, encourage them to stop and join in again when they 'feel' the pulse.

Extension Activities

Work in pairs with one ball, the children bouncing the ball between them. How long can they keep in time to the music?

Try the activity using skipping ropes instead, the rope tapping the floor to the pulse as they skip.

Discuss and share playground skipping games that the children know.

Music Attainment Target: 1 & 2
Main Focus: Listening and Pulse
Key Stage: 1/2

P.E. Attainment Target: 1
Main Focus: Ball Skills

Rollerball

Suggested Materials

One ball per pair of children.

Suggested Listening

Extracts of music with a strong beat (e.g. pop music, swing, Latin American or marching music).

1. The children work in pairs. Each pair has a ball which they will roll across the floor to each other. The children kneel facing each other, 1½ – 2 metres apart.
2. Play the music to the children. They roll the ball to each other attempting to time the arrival of the ball at their partner in time with the music.
3. Songs can also be used in this activity. Below is an example of how the rollerball can be used with 'The Grand Old Duke of York'.

Oh the Grand old Duke of York
(roll........................collect)

he had ten thousand men
(roll.....................collect)

he marched them up to the top of the hill,
(roll...............................collect)

and he marched them down again.
(roll...........................collect)

Music Attainment Target: 2
Main Focus: Appraising and Pulse
Key Stage: 2

P.E. Attainment Target: 1
Main Focus: Co-ordination

Scramble

Suggested Materials

Tuned percussion, chime bars, five or six pieces of untuned percussion.

1. This is a version of a well-known team game which incorporates acute listening into the activity.
2. The class is divided up into equal teams, who sit down in lines at one end of the hall. Each child in the team is allocated a sound, e.g.

   Child 1 in each group is given the sound of a triangle
   Child 2 in each group is given the sound of claves, etc.
3. Use one of the teams to play the instruments. They must stand behind the other teams so that the children cannot see which instrument is being played.
4. With the teacher indicating which instrument is to be played, the children must listen for the sound allocated to them. If it is played they get up and run (or hop, skip, jump, etc.) to the other end of the hall, as fast as they can. The team whose member gets back first receives a point.
5. The sounds used can vary and can increase the difficulty of the activity.
   - Contrasting sounds – claves, drum, tambourine, triangle, etc.
   - Similar sounds – Yoghurt pots filled with rice, sand, pasta, etc.

Extension Activities

Possible sequences for older children:

Untuned percussion	**Tuned percussion**
Child 1 – tambour, tambour, triangle	Child 1 – low, low, high
Child 2 – tambour, triangle, tambour	Child 2 – low, high, low
Child 3 – bells, triangle, tambour	Child 3 – high, high, low

Music Attainment Target: 2
Main Focus: Appraising
Key Stage: 1/2

P.E. Attainment Target: 1
Main Focus: Games

Make a Folk Dance

Suggested Materials

Recording of country dance music (including folk dance music from other countries).

1. Country dancing is an excellent way for children to understand and 'feel' rhythm and musical phrasing.
2. Listen with the children to a piece of country dance music. Clap along to it. How many claps are there in each phrase? It will usually divide into groups of eight.
3. Now begin to devise your dance with the children. Build up gradually using very simple movements. It is probably easiest to start with the children in a circle all doing the same movements.

   Below are some suggestions:

   8 steps to the right
   8 steps to the left
   4 steps forwards, 4 steps backwards
   With a partner, swing 4 times to the right and 4 times to the left.
   3 steps to the middle, clap, 3 steps back, clap.

4. Try using folk music from other countries, e.g. American square dance, Irish jig, Israeli and Greek folk dance, etc.

Extension Activities

The children may come up with other ideas, and you could extend this by asking them to choreograph their own folk dance together in groups. Always encourage them to listen carefully and match their movements to the phrasing of the music.

Music Attainment Target: 2
Main Focus: Pulse and Phrasing
Key Stage: 1/2

P.E. Attainment Target: 1
Main Focus: Dance

Warm Up

Suggested Listening

Recording of 'disco' type music.

1. Build up a sequence of exercises with the children over several P.E. sessions, ending up with a complete exercise routine which the children know well and can use automatically at the beginning of each session.
2. It is important to start with small movements using individual parts of the body, gradually extending to large, whole-body movements.

   Example of an exercise routine:

   a) open and close fists (x8)
   b) swivel right wrist (x4)
   c) swivel left wrist (x4)
   d) swivel both wrists (x8)
   e) shrug both shoulders (x8)
   f) swing arms forward (x8)
   g) march on the spot (x8)
   h) march and swing arms (x8)
   i) touch toes (x8)
   j) star jumps (x8)

The children may devise their own routines in groups which they could then perform to the rest of the class.

Encourage careful listening and rhythmic response to the music.

Music Attainment Target: 2
Main Focus: Pulse and Phrasing
Key Stage: 1/2

P.E. Attainment Target: 1
Main Focus: Movement

Mirror Mirror

Suggested Listening

Recorded extracts of expressive music (e.g. 'Canon' by Pachelbel, 'Air' from *Suite No. 3 in D* by J.S. Bach, 'The Swan' from *Carnival of the Animals* by Saint-Saëns, 'Walking in the Air' from *The Snowman* by Howard Blake, *Trois Gymnopédies* by Satie).

1. The children stand in pairs facing each other. They choose who is to be the leader, and who is going to be the reflection.
2. The leader (remaining in his/her place) responds to the music using arm movements, e.g.

   gliding, high, low, falling, swirling, slow, smooth, jerky.
3. The 'reflector' must try to follow the movements of the leader. (This is a good activity for concentrating on slow, expressive music.)
4. Swap over so that the leader is now the reflection.
5. Discuss the features of the extracts of music with the children. What was the mood? What was the pace? What instruments were used? What dynamics (loud, quiet, etc.) were involved? Which pieces did they like?

Music Attainment Target: 2 Main Focus: Appraising Key Stage: 2	P.E. Attainment Target: 1 Main Focus: Movement

The Hidden Doorway

Suggested Materials

A blindfold. Vocal sounds. (A variety of percussion for the extension activity)

1. The children each decide on an individual vocal sound they can make. Each sound must be different. (It is useful to have a back-up of suggestions for reticent children, e.g. a cough, sneeze, hiccup, laugh, surprised grunt, snore, word, etc.)
2. Now choose two children to share the same sound, and a third to be blindfolded.
3. The rest of the class form a circle.
4. Quietly place the two children with the same sound side by side, and slightly apart in the circle. These two children form the 'Hidden Doorway' into the circle.
5. The blindfolded child walks round the outside of the circle, while all the other children make their vocal sounds. By listening carefully, he or she must find the 'Hidden Doorway' and walk through it into the circle.

Extension Activities

Try the same activity with percussion, all but two of the children having different instruments.

Music Attainment Target: 2
Main Focus: Listening
Key Stage: 2

P.E. Attainment Target: 1
Main Focus: Spatial Awareness

Twister

Suggested Materials

Drum or tambour.

1. On a drum play a slow, steady beat. Ask the children to walk round to this, stepping on every beat.

2. As they walk, ask them to count to four, over and over again (i.e. '1 2 3 4, 1 2 3 4, 1 2 3 4, 1 2 3 4').

3. Repeat the activity, but this time they must change direction every time they say '1'.

(ch = change)

```
1 2 3 4 1 2 3 4 1 2 3 4 1 2 3 4 1 2 3 4
ch      ch      ch      ch      ch
```

4. Can the children stamp on beat 1, when they change direction?

5. Repeat using other number patterns, e.g. 1–3, 1–5, 1–6, and so on.

Music Attainment Target: 2
Main Focus: Appraising and Pulse
Key Stage: 2

P.E. Attainment Target: 1
Main Focus: Movement

Get Together

Suggested Materials

Drum, tambour or claves.

1. Play a slow, steady beat on one of the above instruments. Having experienced the previous activity, extend by gradually adding other actions. (Counting aloud will help.) For example:

Pattern of 6

1	2	3	4	5	6
stamp		click fingers		reach up	

Pattern of 8

1	2	3	4	5	6	7	8
bend	click fingers		clap				turn

2. Having practised all these patterns individually, divide the class in two. Can one group maintain a pattern of 6 while the other keeps a pattern of 8? (This will take a lot of concentration.)

Extension Activities

Extend to using other patterns as well, e.g. 3, 5 and 7. How many patterns can the children maintain against each other?

Music Attainment Target: 2
Main Focus: Appraising and Pulse
Key Stage: 2

P.E. Attainment Target: 1
Main Focus: Co-ordination

Choreography

Suggested Materials

A variety of percussion. Audio tape-recorder.

1. Ask the children, in groups, to build up a sequence of sounds on a variety of instruments. Encourage the children to use patterns on the instruments rather than just single sounds, and to use contrasts, e.g.

   slow/fast, loud/quiet, long/short, high/low.

2. Groups practise playing their sequences, concentrating on developing fluency in going from one part of the sequence to the next.
3. Groups perform their sequences to each other while the teacher records them on separate audio tapes.
4. The children listen to their sequences on tape and discuss how these sounds could be translated into movement which would reflect the contrasts in the sound sequences.
5. The groups then build up a movement sequence to match their taped sequence.

Music Attainment Target: 1
Main Focus: Composing
Key Stage: 2

P.E. Attainment Target: 1
Main Focus: Dance

Sound Moves

Suggested Materials

Access to a variety of percussion.

1. Discuss with the children possible contrasts in movement:

fast/slow
sudden/sustained
high/low
narrow/wide
rhythmic/free
heavy/light.

2. Ask the children, in groups, to put together a sequence of contrasting movements. Encourage them to aim for a controlled and fluent performance of their sequence.

3. Having performed their movement sequences to each other, ask the children to produce a 'soundtrack' to match. Encourage them to think very carefully about what instruments to use and how best to play them in order to reflect the characteristics of the movements involved.

Music Attainment Target: 1
Main Focus: Composing
Key Stage: 2

P.E. Attainment Target: 1
Main Focus: Dance

Appendix

Glossary

Crescendo	Getting louder.
Decrescendo	Getting quieter.
Drone	One or more notes maintained throughout a piece.
Dynamics	The gradations of volume in music.
Form	The order in which different ideas appear in a piece of music.
Improvisation	Composing spontaneously while performing.
Glissando	The process of moving from one note to another quickly, while playing all other notes in between.
Notation	The symbolic written representation of sound(s).
Ostinato	A rhythm or melody pattern repeated regularly during a piece of music (often as accompaniment).
Pitch	The perception of sounds as 'high' or 'low' in relation to each other. A woman's voice is usually higher in pitch than a man's.
Pulse	A repetitive, regular beat (sometimes silent), which can indicate the speed of a piece of music.
Rest	'Musical silence' – the absence of a sounding note or notes.
Rhythm	The pattern which long and short sounds and rests make when heard in sequence.
Rhythmic independence	The ability to maintain a rhythm against other rhythms.
Score	A written record of all the parts in a piece of music.
Sequencing	The ordering of sounds.
Timbre	The characteristics/colour of sound(s).
Volume	The loudness or quietness of sound/music.

Symbols

f	Loud
p	Quiet
<	Getting louder
>	Getting quieter

Pentatonic Scales

The notes on tuned percussion should be arranged with long bars to the left, getting increasingly smaller to the right-hand side, and in alphabetical order. Most (but not all) start with 'C'.

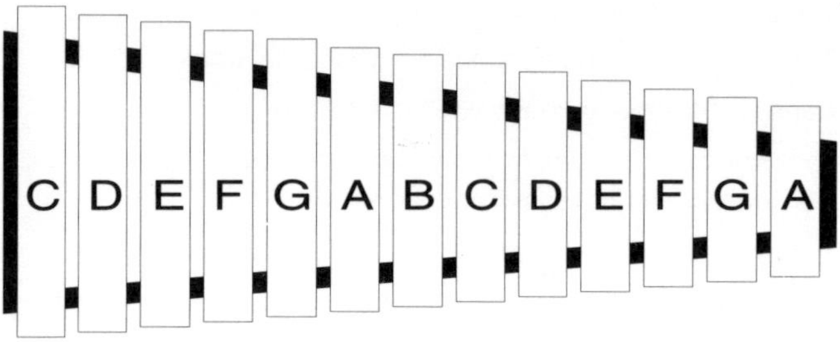

By removing any note 'B' and any note 'F', it is possible to have a five-note scale, called 'Pentatonic' (Penta = five). This should leave a sequence of C D E G A.

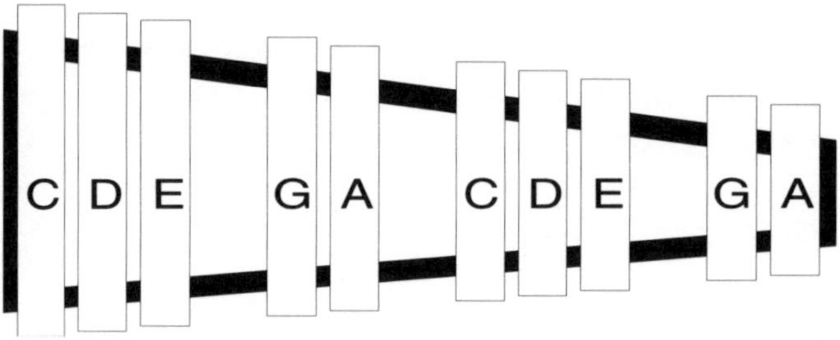

A pentatonic scale is useful for improvising melodies, both solo and in group work.

Occasionally instruments will come with notes called 'sharps' (with a ♯ after the letter), and 'flats' (with a ♭ after the letter), e.g. C♯ E♭ F♯ G♯ B♭. By using only these notes, it is again possible to create a pentatonic scale. This same scale can be found by just using the black notes on a piano or keyboard. Use this scale if most of the notes on your tuned percussion are sharps and flats.

Teacher's Notes

Teacher's Notes